contents

recipes	2
glossary	60
conversion chart	62
index	63

NZ, Canada, US and UK readers
Please note that Australian cup and
spoon measurements are metric.
A conversion chart appears on page 62.

chorizo taquitos with chilli tomato salsa

You need 40 toothpicks with two-pointed ends for this recipe.

450g can refried beans
1 tablespoon water
400g chorizo sausage, chopped finely
½ medium red capsicum (100g), chopped finely
3 green onions, chopped finely
10 large flour tortillas, cut into quarters
vegetable oil, for deep-frying

chilli tomato salsa
425g can peeled tomatoes
2 fresh small red thai chillies, seeded, quartered
1 clove garlic, quartered
⅓ cup loosely packed fresh coriander leaves
1 small brown onion (80g), cut into quarters

1 Heat beans with the water in small saucepan.
2 Meanwhile, make chilli tomato salsa.
3 Cook chorizo in large frying pan, stirring, until crisp; drain on absorbent paper.
4 Combine bean mixture and chorizo in medium bowl with capsicum and onion. Divide filling among tortilla pieces; roll each taquito into cone shape, secure with toothpick.
5 Heat oil in large saucepan; deep-fry taquitos, in batches, until browned lightly and crisp. Drain on absorbent paper. Remove toothpicks.
6 Serve hot taquitos with salsa.

chilli tomato salsa Blend or process ingredients until just combined.

makes 40
preparation time 40 minutes
cooking time 15 minutes
per taquito 5.2g fat; 337kJ (80 cal)
per tablespoon salsa 0g fat; 17kJ (4 cal)

chicken enchiladas with corn salsa

1 large red onion (300g),
   chopped finely
2 tablespoons vegetable oil
2 cloves garlic, crushed
1 tablespoon tomato paste
¼ cup (45g) drained bottled
   jalapeño chillies,
     chopped coarsely
400g can crushed tomatoes
1 cup (250ml) chicken stock
500g chicken breast fillets,
   sliced thinly
10 corn tortillas
2 cups (250g) coarsely grated
   cheddar cheese
½ cup (120g) sour cream

corn salsa
1 small red capsicum (150g),
   chopped finely
310g can corn kernels, drained
1 tablespoon lime juice
1 cup coarsely chopped
   fresh coriander

1 Preheat oven to 180°C/160°C fan-forced.
2 Reserve a quarter of the onion for the corn salsa. Heat oil in large frying pan; cook remaining onion with garlic, stirring, until onion softens. Add tomato paste, chilli, undrained tomatoes, stock and chicken; bring to a boil. Reduce heat; simmer, uncovered, until chicken is cooked through. Remove chicken from pan; cover to keep warm.
3 Soften tortillas according to manufacturer's instructions. Dip tortillas, one at a time, in tomato mixture in pan; place on board. Divide chicken and half of the cheese among tortillas, placing along edge; roll tortilla to enclose filling. Place enchiladas, seam-side down, in large oiled 3-litre (12-cup) shallow ovenproof dish; enchiladas should fit snugly, without overcrowding.
4 Pour remaining tomato mixture over enchiladas; top with sour cream, sprinkle with remaining cheese. Bake, uncovered, in oven about 15 minutes or until heated through.
5 Meanwhile, make corn salsa.
6 Divide enchiladas among serving plates; serve with corn salsa.
corn salsa Place reserved onion, capsicum, corn, juice and coriander in small bowl; toss to combine.

serves 4
preparation time 30 minutes
cooking time 35 minutes
per serving 51.6g fat; 3152kJ (753 cal)

salt and pepper prawns

You need to soak 18 small bamboo skewers in water for an hour before use, to prevent them from splintering and scorching.

18 uncooked king prawns (1kg)
2 teaspoons sea salt
¼ teaspoon chilli powder
½ teaspoon freshly ground black pepper

1 Shell and devein prawns, leaving tails intact; thread prawns onto skewers lengthways.
2 Combine remaining ingredients in small bowl; cook prawns, in batches, sprinkling with half the salt mixture, on heated oiled grill plate (or grill or barbecue) until browned all over and cooked through.
3 Serve prawns with separate bowl of remaining salt mixture.

serves 6
preparation time 20 minutes
cooking time 5 minutes
per serving 0.5g fat; 311kJ (74 cal)

chile con carne with jalapeño corn muffins

1 cup (200g) dried kidney beans
1.5kg beef chuck steak
2 litres (8 cups) water
1 tablespoon olive oil
2 medium brown onions (300g), chopped coarsely
2 cloves garlic, crushed
2 teaspoons ground cumin
2 teaspoons ground coriander
½ teaspoon ground cayenne pepper
2 teaspoons sweet paprika
2 x 400g cans crushed tomatoes
1 tablespoon tomato paste
4 green onions, chopped coarsely
2 tablespoons finely chopped fresh coriander
⅓ cup (65g) finely chopped bottled jalapeño chillies

jalapeño corn muffins
1 cup (150g) plain flour
1 teaspoon baking powder
2 cups (340g) polenta
2 teaspoons salt
1 cup (250ml) milk
2 cups (500ml) buttermilk
2 tablespoons olive oil
2 eggs, beaten lightly
1⅓ cups (165g) finely grated cheddar cheese
⅓ cup (65g) finely chopped bottled jalapeño chillies

1 Place beans in medium bowl, cover with water; soak overnight, drain.

2 Combine beef and the water in large pan; bring to a boil; simmer, covered, 1½ hours, cool slightly.

3 Drain meat in large muslin-lined strainer placed over bowl; reserve 3½ cups of the cooking liquid. Using two forks, shred beef.

4 Heat oil in same pan; cook brown onion and garlic, stirring, until onion is soft. Add spices; cook, stirring, until fragrant. Add undrained tomatoes, beans, paste and 2 cups of the reserved cooking liquid; bring to a boil. Reduce heat; simmer, covered, 1 hour.

5 Meanwhile, make jalapeño corn muffins.

6 Add beef and remaining reserved cooking liquid to pan; simmer, covered, about 30 minutes or until beans are tender.

7 Just before serving, stir in green onion, coriander and chilli. Serve with muffins.

jalapeño corn muffins Preheat oven to 180°C/160°C fan-forced. Grease 12-hole ½-cup (125ml) muffin pan. Sift flour and baking powder into large bowl; stir in remaining ingredients until just combined. Spoon mixture into pan holes. Bake, uncovered, 35 minutes.

serves 8
preparation time 25 minutes
(plus standing time)
cooking time 3 hours 30 minutes
per serving 11.7g fat; 1290kJ (308 cal)
per muffin 16.7g fat; 1715kJ (409 cal)

empanadas

Empanadas are sweet or savoury turnovers made from flaky pastry. Our quick savoury version uses ready-rolled puff pastry sheets.

1 tablespoon vegetable oil
1 small brown onion (80g), chopped coarsely
2 small tomatoes (260g), seeded, chopped coarsely
1 small green capsicum (150g), chopped coarsely
2 tablespoons drained, thinly sliced, seeded black olives
2 tablespoons coarsely chopped fresh flat-leaf parsley
3 sheets ready-rolled puff pastry, thawed
1½ cups (185g) coarsely grated cheddar cheese

1 Heat oil in medium frying pan; cook onion, tomato, capsicum and olives, stirring, until tomato just begins to soften. Remove from heat; stir through parsley. Allow filling to cool.
2 Preheat oven to 200°C/180°C fan-forced. Using 11cm-round cutter, cut four rounds from each pastry sheet.
3 Divide tomato filling among pastry rounds; top with equal amounts of cheese. Fold over pastry to enclose filling; pinch edges together to seal. Using knife, make two 1cm cuts in top of each pastry.
4 Place empanadas on greased oven tray; bake 15 minutes or until golden. Serve with avocado salsa, if desired.

makes 12
preparation time 15 minutes
cooking time 20 minutes (plus cooling time)
per empanada 16.3g fat; 934kJ (223 cal)

bean nachos

Mexican-style beans are a mildly spiced, canned combination of red kidney or pinto beans, capsicum and tomato.

420g canned mexican-style beans, drained
290g canned kidney beans, rinsed, drained, mashed
2 tablespoons tomato paste
1 tablespoon water
230g packet plain corn chips
1½ cups (185g) coarsely grated cheddar cheese
1 large avocado (320g)
1 teaspoon lemon juice
1 small red onion (100g), chopped finely
1 large tomato (250g), chopped finely
½ cup (120g) sour cream
1 tablespoon coarsely chopped fresh coriander

1 Preheat oven to 200°C/180°C fan-forced.
2 Heat combined beans, paste and the water, stirring, in large oiled frying pan. Cover to keep warm.
3 Place corn chips in large ovenproof dish; sprinkle with cheese. Bake in oven 5 minutes or until cheese melts.
4 Meanwhile, mash avocado in small bowl; stir in juice and half the combined onion and tomato.
5 Top heated corn chips with bean mixture, avocado mixture and sour cream; sprinkle nachos with remaining onion and tomato, and coriander.

serves 4
preparation time 10 minutes
cooking time 10 minutes
per serving 60g fat; 3840kJ (917 cal)
tips Drizzle sweet chilli sauce over sour cream for a spicy alternative. Corn chips are available in a variety of flavours, any of which can be substituted for the plain variety.

corn and zucchini fritters with salsa

50g butter, melted
½ cup (125ml) milk
¾ cup (110g) plain flour
2 eggs, beaten lightly
210g can creamed corn
2 medium zucchini (240g), grated coarsely
vegetable oil, for shallow-frying
salsa
3 medium egg tomatoes (225g), chopped coarsely
2 medium avocados (500g), chopped coarsely
1 small red onion (100g), chopped coarsely
2 tablespoons lime juice
2 tablespoons finely chopped fresh coriander

1 Make salsa.
2 Combine butter, milk, flour and egg in medium bowl; whisk until smooth. Add corn and zucchini; mix well.
3 Heat oil in medium frying pan; cook heaped tablespoons of batter, one at a time, about 2 minutes each side or until browned both sides and cooked through. Drain on absorbent paper. Serve with salsa.
salsa Combine ingredients in small bowl.

serves 4
preparation time 10 minutes
cooking time 10 minutes
per serving 57.6g fat; 2922kJ (698 cal)

chickpea corn **enchiladas**

We used 16cm-round corn tortillas, which are cryovac packaged. Unused tortillas can be frozen in freezer bags for up to three weeks.

1 tablespoon olive oil
1 small brown onion (80g), chopped coarsely
1 clove garlic, crushed
1 teaspoon sweet paprika
½ teaspoon ground chilli powder
1 teaspoon ground cumin
400g can tomato puree
300g can chickpeas, rinsed, drained
1 tablespoon coarsely chopped fresh coriander
8 corn tortillas
1 small red onion (100g), chopped coarsely
1 medium tomato (190g), chopped coarsely
1 small avocado (200g), chopped coarsely
½ cup (60g) coarsely grated cheddar cheese
½ cup finely shredded iceberg lettuce

1 Heat oil in medium saucepan; cook brown onion and garlic, stirring, until onion softens. Add spices; cook, stirring, 2 minutes. Add puree, bring to a boil; reduce heat, simmer, stirring occasionally, 5 minutes. Add chickpeas and coriander; cook, stirring, until hot.
2 Soften tortillas in microwave oven on HIGH (100%) for 30 seconds. Divide chickpea mixture and remaining ingredients among tortillas; fold enchiladas to enclose filling.

serves 4
preparation time 15 minutes
cooking time 10 minutes
per serving 21.2g fat; 1972kJ (471 cal)
tip You can also soften tortillas by wrapping them in foil and heating them in a moderate oven for about 5 minutes or until hot.

chile con frijoles

Mexican-style beans are a mildly spiced, canned combination of red kidney or pinto beans, capsicum and tomato.

1 tablespoon olive oil
1 large red onion (300g), chopped coarsely
1½ teaspoons ground cumin
1 fresh small red thai chilli, chopped finely
1 small red capsicum (150g), chopped coarsely
420g can Mexican-style beans
1¼ cups (375ml) water
2 tablespoons tomato paste
310g can corn kernels rinsed, drained
1 medium tomato (190g), chopped coarsely
2 teaspoons lime juice
¼ cup finely chopped fresh coriander

1 Heat oil in large saucepan. Add onion, cumin and chilli; cook, stirring, 3 minutes or until onion softens.
2 Add capsicum, undrained beans, the water and paste; bring to a boil. Reduce heat; simmer, stirring, 5 minutes or until bean mixture thickens slightly.
3 Add corn, tomato, juice and coriander; cook, stirring, until hot.
4 Serve with sour cream and plain or flavoured corn chips, if desired.

serves 4
preparation time 10 minutes
cooking time 10 minutes
per serving 6.2g fat; 1059kJ (253 cal)

prawn fritters with avocado salsa

450g cooked large prawns
2 tablespoons olive oil
1 medium brown onion (150g), chopped coarsely
1 clove garlic, crushed
2 teaspoons hot paprika
½ teaspoon ground cumin
¼ teaspoon ground white pepper
¼ teaspoon cayenne pepper
1½ cups (225g) self-raising flour
2 eggs
1½ cups (375ml) milk
1 tablespoon coarsely chopped fresh chives
2 medium avocados (500g), chopped coarsely
2 medium tomatoes (380g), chopped coarsely
1 spring onion (25g), sliced thinly
2 tablespoons lime juice

1 Shell and devein prawns; chop prawn flesh coarsely.
2 Heat half the oil in large frying pan; cook onion, garlic and spices, stirring, until onion softens.
3 Place flour in large bowl; stir in combined eggs and milk, stir until smooth. Stir in chives, onion mixture and prawn.
4 Heat remaining oil in cleaned frying pan; cook ¼ cups of prawn mixture, in batches, until browned both sides.
5 Meanwhile, combine remaining ingredients in medium bowl. Serve fritters with avocado salsa.

serves 4
preparation time 20 minutes
cooking time 10 minutes
per serving 36.7g fat; 2625kJ (627 cal)
tips Fritter batter can be prepared four hours ahead; cover, refrigerate. You can buy 200g of shelled prawns, if you prefer, for this recipe.

mexican beef

750g beef rump steak, sliced thinly
35g packet taco seasoning
2 tablespoons peanut oil
1 large red onion (300g), sliced thinly
1 medium red capsicum (200g), sliced thinly
1 medium yellow capsicum (200g), sliced thinly
4 small tomatoes (520g), chopped coarsely
¼ cup coarsely chopped fresh coriander

1 Combine beef and seasoning in large bowl. Heat half the oil in wok; stir-fry beef and onion, in batches, until browned.
2 Heat remaining oil in wok; stir-fry capsicums until just tender.
3 Combine beef mixture, capsicums, tomatoes and coriander in large bowl. Serve with flour tortillas, if desired.

serves 4
preparation time 10 minutes
cooking time 15 minutes
per serving 19.3g fat; 1704kJ (407 cal)

spinach and cheese quesadillas

Quesadillas are filled tortillas that are grilled or fried and served with fresh salsa. We used small flour tortillas measuring approximately 16cm in diameter; they are sometimes labelled "fajita tortillas" on the package.

⅔ cup (130g) low-fat cottage cheese
100g spinach leaves, trimmed
1 medium avocado (230g), chopped finely
1 cup (200g) canned Mexican-style beans, drained
125g can corn kernels, rinsed, drained
2 medium tomatoes (380g), seeded, chopped finely
1 small red onion (100g), chopped finely
2 medium zucchini (240g), grated coarsely
16 small flour tortillas
1½ cups (150g) coarsely grated mozzarella cheese

1 Blend or process cottage cheese and spinach until smooth.
2 Combine avocado, beans, corn, tomato, onion and zucchini in medium bowl.
3 Place eight tortillas on lightly oiled oven tray; divide spinach mixture among tortillas, leaving 2cm border around edge. Divide avocado mixture among tortillas by sprinkling over spinach mixture. Top each with one of the remaining tortillas.
4 Preheat grill. Sprinkle mozzarella over quesadilla stacks; place under grill until cheese just melts and browns lightly.

serves 8
preparation time 20 minutes
cooking time 10 minutes
per serving 11.2g fat; 1155kJ (275 cal)

beef fajitas

You need a small iceberg lettuce for this recipe and two packets of small flour tortillas measuring 16cm in diameter (sometimes labelled "fajita tortillas" on the package).

800g trimmed beef rump steak
1 large red capsicum (350g), sliced thinly
1 large green capsicum (350g), sliced thinly
1 large yellow capsicum (350g), sliced thinly
1 large red onion (300g), sliced thinly
16 small flour tortillas
3 cups finely shredded iceberg lettuce
1¼ cups (155g) coarsely grated cheddar cheese

fresh tomato salsa
3 medium tomatoes (570g), seeded, chopped finely
1 medium red onion (170g), chopped finely
1 tablespoon finely chopped drained jalapeño chillies
¼ cup finely chopped fresh coriander
1 tablespoon lemon juice

1 Heat large lightly oiled grill plate (or grill or barbecue). Sear beef both sides until browned and cooked as desired. Cover; stand 10 minutes. Slice thinly.
2 Meanwhile, make fresh tomato salsa.
3 Cook capsicums and onion on grill plate until vegetables are browned all over.
4 Heat tortillas according to manufacturer's instructions on package.
5 Divide beef slices and vegetables among tortillas on serving plates. Top each with lettuce and cheese; roll to enclose filling. Serve with fresh tomato salsa.
fresh tomato salsa Combine ingredients in small bowl.

serves 8
preparation time 30 minutes
cooking time 20 minutes
per serving 9g fat; 1390kJ (332 cal)

penne with chile con carne

375g penne
1 tablespoon peanut oil
1 large brown onion (200g), sliced thinly
2 cloves garlic, crushed
2 fresh small red thai chillies, chopped coarsely
1 teaspoon ground cumin
1 teaspoon ground coriander
350g yellow teardrop tomatoes, halved
500g thinly sliced roast beef
420g can kidney beans, drained, rinsed
600ml bottled tomato pasta sauce
⅓ cup loosely packed fresh coriander leaves

1 Cook pasta in large saucepan of boiling water, uncovered, until just tender; drain.
2 Meanwhile, heat oil in large saucepan; cook onion, garlic, chilli and spices, stirring, until onion softens. Add tomato; cook, stirring, until tomato is just soft. Add beef, beans and sauce; bring to a boil. Reduce heat; simmer, uncovered, until sauce thickens slightly.
3 Place pasta in pan with chile con carne; toss gently over heat until combined and hot. Stir in fresh coriander.

serves 4
preparation time 8 minutes
cooking time 20 minutes
per serving 12.1g fat; 2853kJ (662 cal)

mexican chicken with
black bean and barley salad

Black beans, also known as turtle beans, are jet black with a tiny white eye; black beans can be found, either packaged or loose, in most greengrocers and delicatessens.

½ cup (100g) dried black beans
2⅓ cups (580ml) chicken stock
1 litre (4 cups) water
¾ cup (165g) pearl barley
35g packet taco
    seasoning mix
4 x 170g chicken breast fillets
1 large red capsicum (350g),
    chopped finely
1 clove garlic, crushed
¼ cup (60ml) lime juice
2 teaspoons olive oil
½ cup loosely packed
    fresh coriander leaves

1 Preheat oven to 200°C/180°C fan-forced.
2 Combine beans with 1 cup of the stock and half the water in medium saucepan; bring to a boil. Reduce heat; simmer, uncovered, about 45 minutes or until tender, drain. Rinse under cold water; drain.
3 Meanwhile, combine barley with 1 cup of the stock and remaining water in medium saucepan; bring to a boil. Reduce heat; simmer, uncovered, until just tender; drain. Rinse under cold water; drain.
4 Blend seasoning with remaining stock in medium bowl, add chicken; toss to coat chicken in mixture. Drain chicken; reserve marinade. Place chicken, in single layer, on metal rack in large shallow baking dish; bake, uncovered, in oven, about 30 minutes or until cooked through, brushing with reserved marinade halfway through cooking time. Cover; stand 5 minutes then slice thickly.
5 Combine beans and barley in large bowl with remaining ingredients. Divide salad among serving plates; top with chicken.

serves 4
preparation time 10 minutes
cooking time 45 minutes
per serving 8.5g fat; 1826kJ (436 cal)

mexican beef salad with fresh corn salsa

4 dried chipotle chillies
⅓ cup (80ml) boiling water
1 medium red onion (150g), chopped coarsely
2 cups (500ml) water, extra
1 tablespoon ground cumin
1 cup (250ml) beef stock
300g piece beef eye fillet, cut into 3mm slices
2 tablespoons light sour cream
½ cup coarsely chopped fresh coriander

fresh corn salsa
1 medium red onion (150g), chopped coarsely
4 cups (660g) fresh corn kernels
2 cloves garlic, crushed
⅓ cup (80ml) lime juice
3 long green chillies, sliced thinly
1 small avocado (200g), chopped coarsely

1 Soak chillies in the boiling water in small heatproof bowl for 10 minutes. When cool enough to handle, remove stalks from chillies; reserve chillies and liquid.
2 Meanwhile, make fresh corn salsa.
3 Cook onion in lightly oiled large frying pan, stirring, until soft. Add the extra water, cumin, stock, chillies and reserved liquid; bring to a boil. Reduce heat; simmer, uncovered, 10 minutes. Using slotted spoon, remove solids from chilli poaching liquid; reserve.
4 Place beef, in single layer, in chilli poaching liquid; turn off heat. Turn beef over; using slotted spoon, remove beef from liquid after 30 seconds. Cover to keep warm.
5 Blend or process reserved solids with cream until almost smooth. Serve beef on salsa; top with chilli cream sauce and sprinkle with coriander.
fresh corn salsa Combine ingredients in medium bowl.

serves 4
preparation time 25 minutes
cooking time 20 minutes
per serving 15g fat; 1564kJ (374 cal)
tips You need four cobs of corn for this recipe. Chipotle are fresh jalapeño chillies that have been dried and smoked. Having a deep, intensely smoky flavour rather than a searing heat, chipotles are dark brown, almost black in appearance; they are available from specialty spice stores and gourmet delicatessens.

enchiladas suizas

400g chicken breast fillets
4 sprigs fresh coriander
6 black peppercorns
¼ cup (45g) chopped bottled jalapeño chillies
2 medium white onions (300g)
¾ cup (180ml) light sour cream
½ cup (75g) pimiento-stuffed green olives, sliced thickly
300g fontina cheese, grated coarsely
12 corn tortillas, softened

fresh tomato salsa
1 tablespoon vegetable oil
1 medium white onion (150g), chopped coarsely
2 cloves garlic, crushed
1 tablespoon finely chopped fresh coriander
3 large tomatoes (750g), seeded, chopped finely
2 tablespoons tomato paste
1 teaspoon mexican seasoning
1 tablespoon finely chopped bottled jalapeño chillies

1 Combine chicken, coriander, peppercorns, half the chilli and 1 halved onion in medium pan with just enough water to cover. Bring to a boil, simmer, covered, about 10 minutes or until chicken is cooked; cool chicken in stock.
2 Drain chicken over large bowl; reserve stock for fresh tomato salsa, discard solids.
3 Make fresh tomato salsa.
4 Shred chicken finely; combine in medium bowl with sour cream, olives, remaining chilli, finely chopped remaining onion and half the cheese.
5 Preheat oven to 200°C/180°C fan-forced.
6 Dip tortilla in fresh tomato salsa, place on board; place ¼ cup chicken mixture on edge of tortilla, roll to enclose filling. Place tortilla, seam-side down, in large (12-cup) oiled shallow ovenproof dish. Repeat with remaining tortillas and chicken mixture.
7 Pour remaining salsa over tortillas; top with remaining cheese. Bake, uncovered, about 20 minutes or until cheese is melted and enchiladas are heated through.

fresh tomato salsa Heat oil in medium saucepan; cook onion and garlic, stirring, until onion is soft. Add remaining ingredients and 1½ cups (375ml) of the reserved chicken stock; simmer about 10 minutes or until tomatoes have softened. Blend or process mixture, in batches, until smooth.

serves 4
preparation time 30 minutes (plus cooling time)
cooking time 40 minutes
per serving 50.1g fat; 3518kJ (840 cal)

sweet paprika chicken
with tomato and chickpea salsa

1.6kg whole chicken
1 tablespoon ground turmeric
2 teaspoons sweet paprika
2 teaspoons finely grated lemon rind
1 clove garlic, crushed
⅓ cup (80ml) olive oil
500g cherry tomatoes
300g can chickpeas, rinsed, drained
⅓ cup coarsely chopped fresh flat-leaf parsley
1 tablespoon lemon juice

1 Wash chicken under cold water; pat dry with absorbent paper. Using kitchen scissors, cut along both sides of backbone; discard backbone. Cut thigh and leg portions from chicken; cut wing portions from chicken. Using knife, slice breast either side of breastbone; discard breastbone. You will have 8 pieces.
2 Combine chicken, turmeric, paprika, rind, garlic and half the oil In large bowl. Cover; refrigerate 3 hours or overnight.
3 Preheat oven to 220°C/200°C fan-forced.
4 Place chicken, in single layer, on wire rack over baking dish; cook, uncovered, about 45 minutes or until chicken is tender.
5 Combine tomatoes and half the remaining oil in baking dish; cook, uncovered, about 15 minutes or until tomatoes are just tender.
6 Just before serving, combine tomatoes, chickpeas, parsley, juice and remaining oil in medium bowl; toss gently. Serve chicken with tomato and chickpea salsa.

serves 4
preparation time 30 minutes (plus refrigeration time)
cooking time 45 minutes
per serving 50.8g fat; 2851kJ (681 cal)

prawn quesadillas
with corn and lime salsa

Corn tortillas are eaten throughout Mexico while flour tortillas, as a rule, mainly play a role in northern Mexican cuisine. Both types are available, fresh or frozen, in most supermarkets.

32 uncooked medium prawns (800g)
2 teaspoons ground cumin
2 teaspoons ground coriander
½ teaspoon chilli powder
1 clove garlic, crushed
1 tablespoon peanut oil
3 green onions, chopped finely
100g fetta cheese, crumbled
8 corn tortillas
½ cup (125ml) sour cream

corn and lime salsa
2 corn cobs (500g)
¼ cup (60ml) lime juice
1 small red onion (100g), chopped finely
4 small tomatoes (520g), seeded, chopped finely
1 medium avocado (250g), chopped coarsely
1 tablespoon coarsely chopped fresh coriander

1 Make corn and lime salsa.
2 Shell and devein prawns; combine in large bowl with cumin, coriander, chilli, garlic and half the oil.
3 Heat remaining oil in large frying pan; cook prawn mixture, in batches, until prawns have changed colour. Combine prawn mixture in large bowl with onion and fetta.
4 Soften tortillas following manufacturer's instructions. Divide prawn mixture among tortillas; fold to enclose quesadilla filling.
5 Place quesadillas, in batches, seam-side down, in same heated pan; cook, uncovered, until browned both sides and heated through.
6 Serve quesadillas with sour cream and corn and lime salsa.

corn and lime salsa Cook corn in heated oiled grill pan (or grill or barbecue) until browned and cooked through. Cut corn kernels from cob; combine in medium bowl with remaining ingredients.

serves 4
preparation time 30 minutes
cooking time 20 minutes
per serving 33.5g fat; 2563kJ (612 cal)

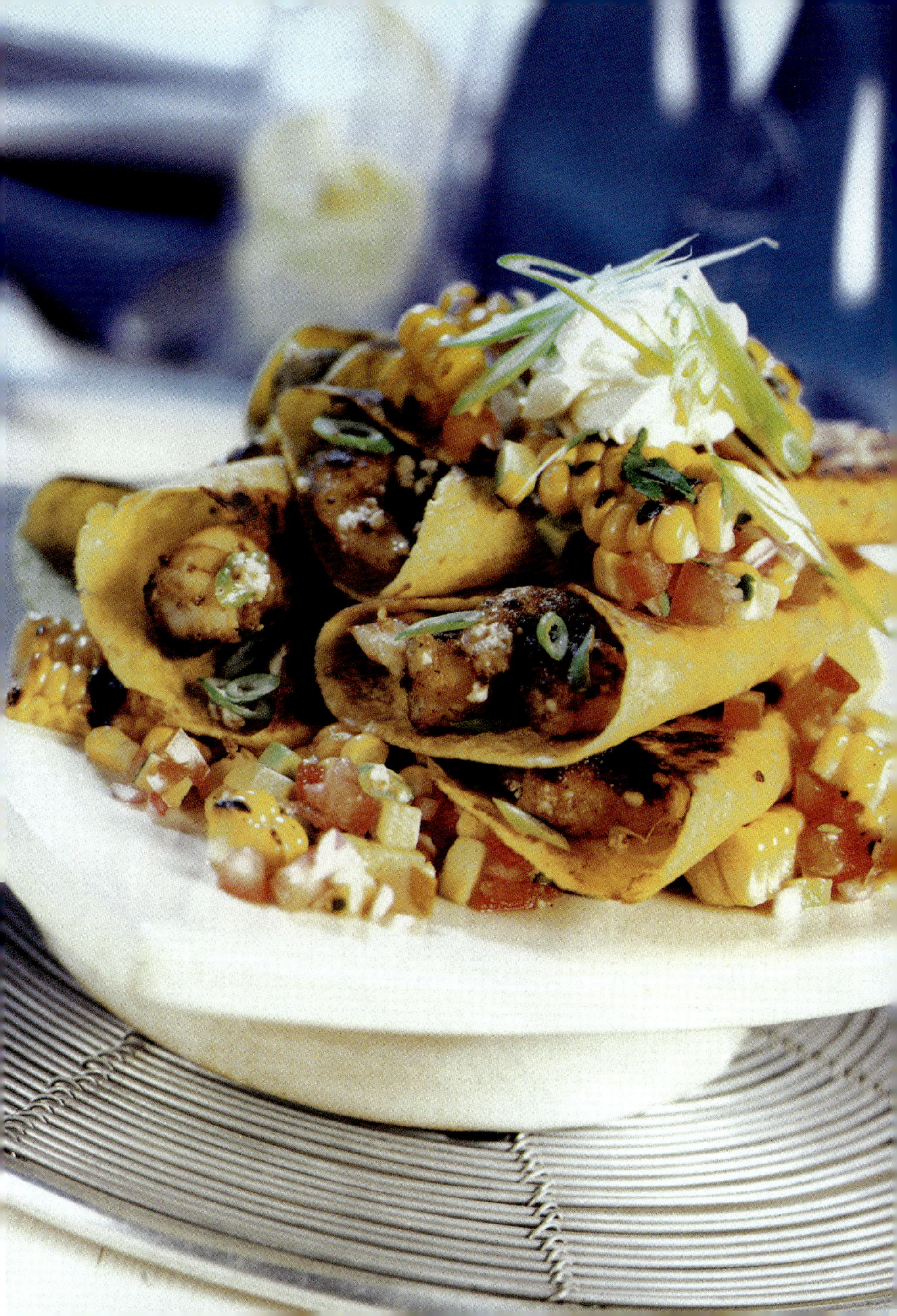

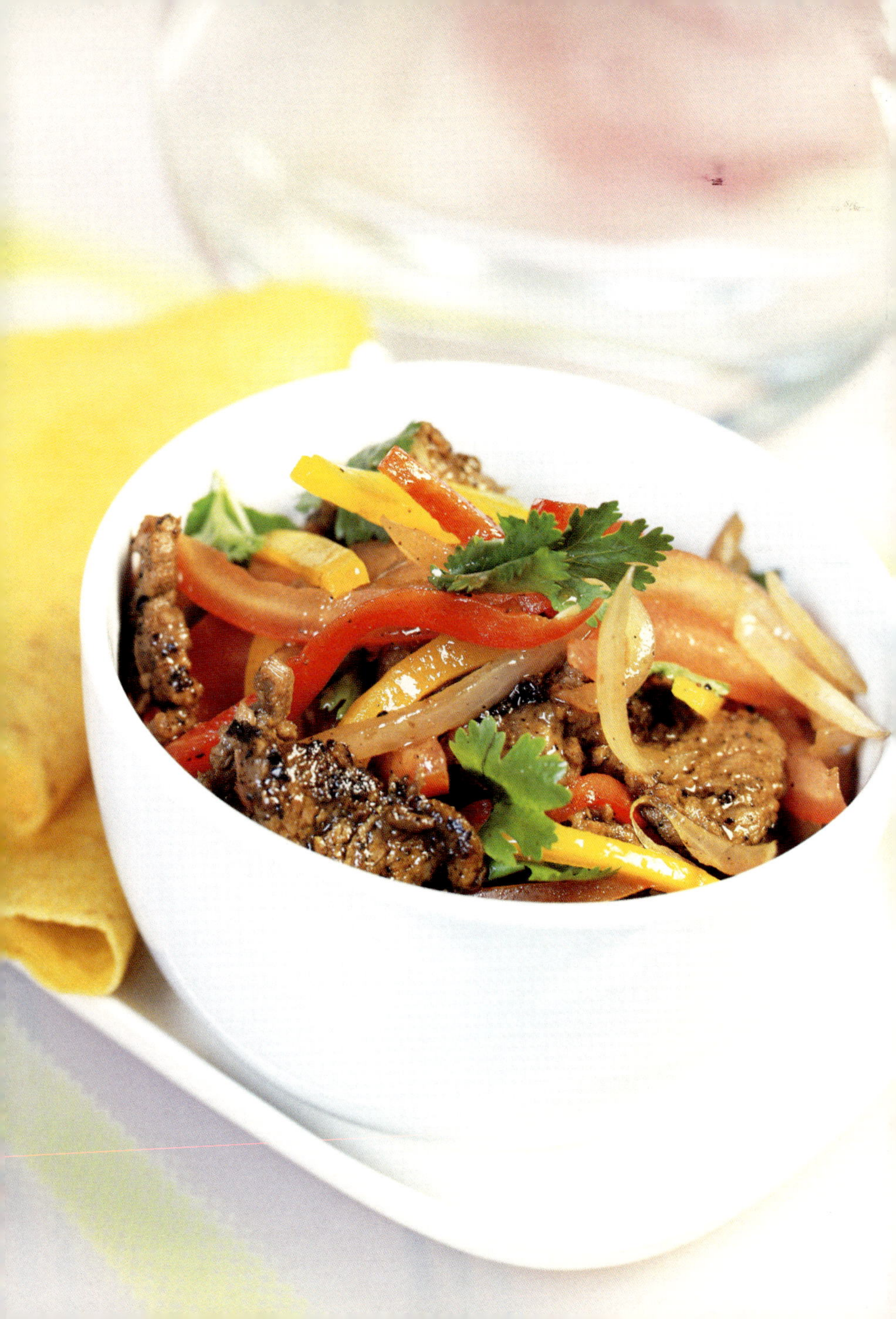

stir-fried mexican beef

750g beef eye fillet, sliced thinly
35g packet taco seasoning
1 tablespoon peanut oil
1 large red onion (300g), sliced thinly
1 medium red capsicum (200g), sliced thinly
1 medium yellow capsicum (200g), sliced thinly
4 small tomatoes (520g), seeded, sliced thinly
2 tablespoons fresh coriander leaves

1 Combine beef and seasoning in medium bowl. Heat half the oil in wok; stir-fry beef mixture and onion, in batches, until well browned.
2 Heat remaining oil in wok; stir-fry capsicums until just tender.
3 Return beef mixture to wok with tomato and coriander; stir-fry until hot.

serves 4
preparation time 20 minutes
cooking time 30 minutes
per serving 13.4g fat; 1449kJ (346 cal)
tip You could also use rib eye (scotch fillet), rump, sirloin or topside in this recipe.

mexican tortilla soup

3 guajillo chillies
¾ cup (180ml) boiling water
2 teaspoons vegetable oil
1 large brown onion (200g), chopped coarsely
3 cloves garlic, crushed
4 medium tomatoes (760g), chopped coarsely
1.5 litres (6 cups) chicken stock
2 tablespoons lime juice
2 cups (500ml) water, extra
350g chicken breast fillets, chopped coarsely
5 corn tortillas
vegetable oil, extra, for shallow-frying
1 small red onion (100g), chopped finely
1 small avocado (200g), chopped finely
1 medium tomato (190g), seeded, chopped finely, extra

1 Remove stems from chillies. Place chillies in small heatproof bowl; cover with the boiling water, stand 10 minutes.
2 Meanwhile, heat oil in large saucepan; cook brown onion and garlic, stirring, until onion is soft. Add tomato and undrained chillies; cook, stirring, about 10 minutes or until tomato is pulpy. Blend or process chilli mixture until pureed.
3 Return chilli mixture to cleaned pan; stir in stock, juice and the extra water. Bring to a boil; add chicken. Simmer, uncovered, about 25 minutes or until chicken is cooked through.
4 Meanwhile, slice tortillas into 1cm strips. Heat extra oil in large frying pan; shallow-fry tortilla strips, in batches, until browned lightly. Drain on absorbent paper.
5 Just before serving, divide soup among serving bowls; sprinkle with tortilla strips and combined red onion, avocado and extra tomato.

serves 6
preparation time 25 minutes
cooking time 45 minutes
per serving 13.4g fat; 1257kJ (300 cal)
tip The guajillo chilli, sometimes called travieso ("impish", because its heat can be deceiving) or cascabel ("little bell", because its dried seeds rattle when the chilli is shaken) is the dried form of the fresh mirasol chilli. So deep-red in colour it is almost black, the medium-hot guajillo chilli must be soaked in boiling water before being used. Any medium-hot dried chilli can be used.

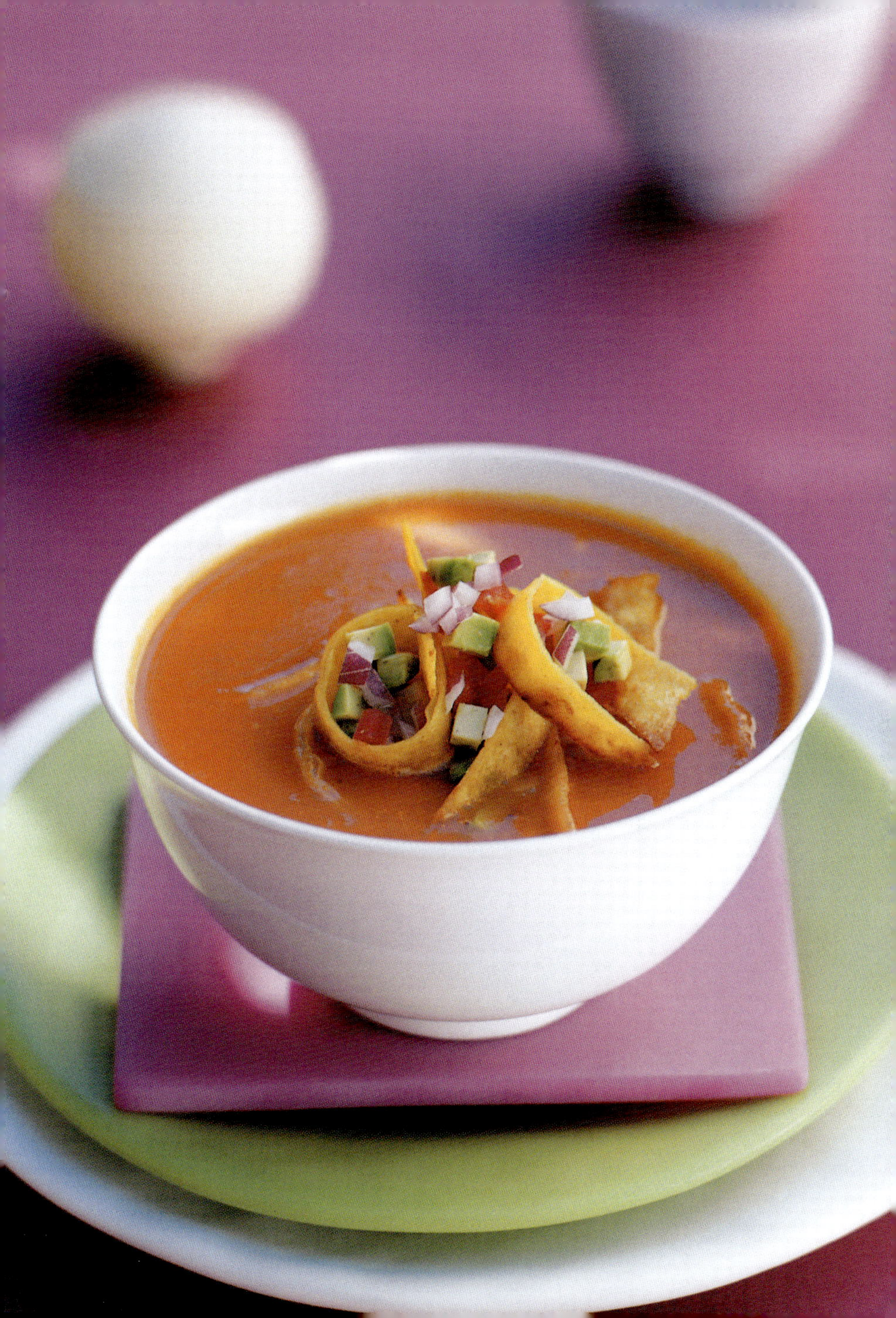

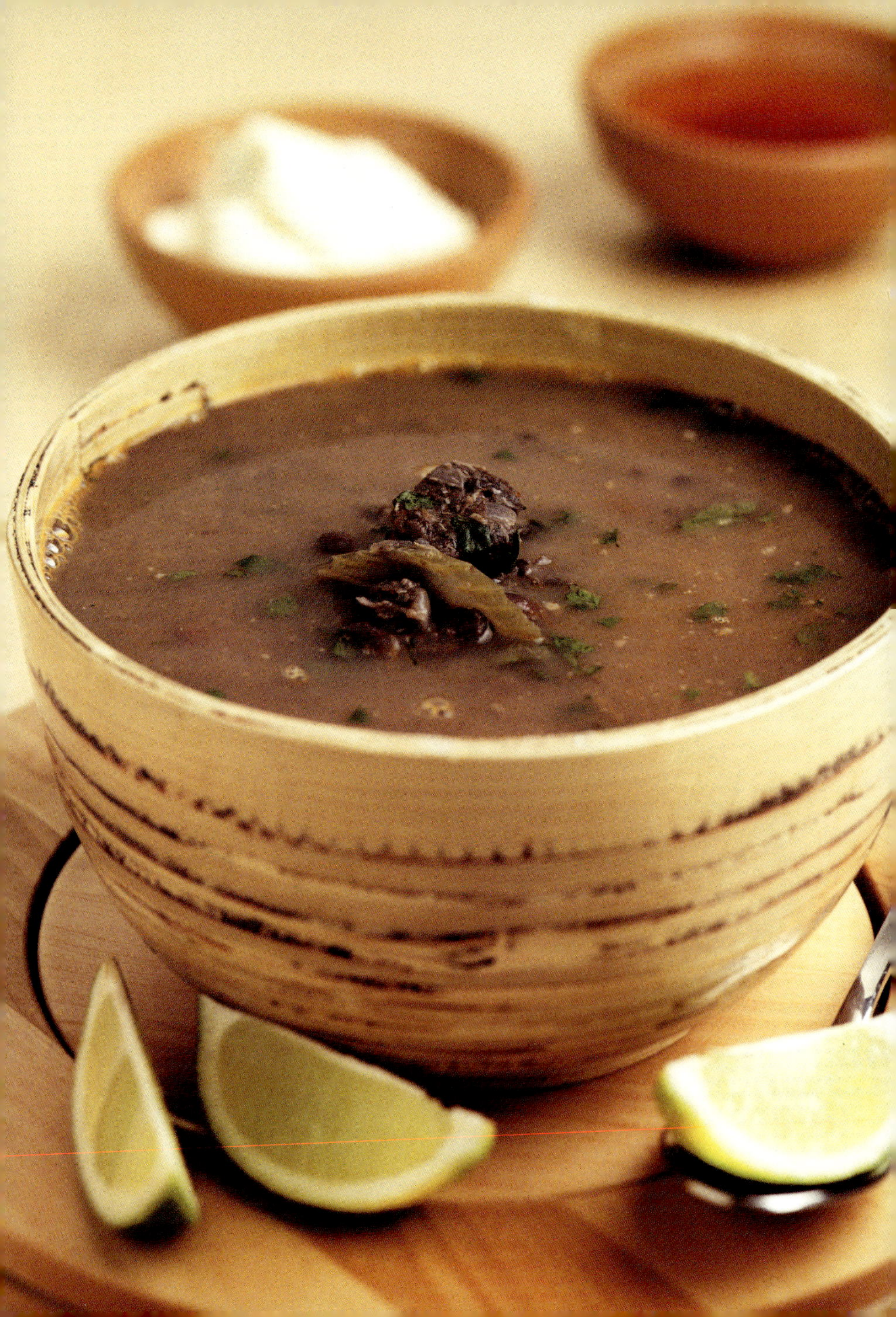

black bean and lamb soup

2 cups (400g) black beans
500g boned lamb shoulder
1 tablespoon olive oil
1 large red onion (300g),
   chopped finely
2 cloves garlic, crushed
2 trimmed celery stalks (200g),
   sliced thinly
1 tablespoon ground cumin
½ teaspoon ground cayenne
2½ litres (10 cups) water
400g can crushed tomatoes
¼ cup (60ml) dry sherry
¼ cup (60ml) balsamic vinegar
¼ cup coarsely chopped
   fresh coriander
4 fresh small red thai chillies,
   chopped finely
⅓ cup (80ml) white
   wine vinegar
½ cup (125ml) sour cream
2 limes, cut into wedges

1 Place beans in medium bowl, cover with water; stand overnight, drain.
2 Trim lamb of excess fat; dice lamb into 1.5cm pieces.
3 Heat oil in large saucepan; cook onion and garlic, stirring, until onion is soft. Add lamb, celery, cumin and cayenne; cook, stirring, about 5 minutes or until spices are just fragrant.
4 Stir in the water and undrained tomatoes; bring to a boil. Reduce heat; simmer, covered, 30 minutes. Add beans; simmer, covered, about 1 hour or until beans are tender. Stir in sherry and balsamic vinegar; cool 10 minutes.
5 Blend or process half the soup, in batches, until pureed.
6 Combine pureed soup with coriander and remaining soup in pan; stir over heat until hot.
7 Combine chilli and white wine vinegar in small bowl. Serve soup accompanied by chilli mixture, sour cream and lime wedges.

serves 6
preparation time 25 minutes
(plus standing time)
cooking time 1 hour 45 minutes
per serving 18.8g fat; 1760kJ (420 cal)

creamed corn and potato patties

800g sebago potatoes
1 corn cob, husk and silk removed
2 egg yolks
310g can creamed corn
¾ cup (45g) fresh breadcrumbs
¼ cup finely chopped fresh flat-leaf parsley
¼ cup (35g) plain flour
50g butter
¼ cup (60ml) vegetable oil

1 Boil, steam or microwave potatoes until tender; drain.
2 Meanwhile, using sharp knife, remove kernels from corn cob.
3 Mash potatoes in large bowl until smooth. Add corn kernels, yolks, creamed corn, breadcrumbs and parsley; stir to combine.
4 Using floured hands, shape mixture into 12 patties. Toss patties in flour, shake away excess. Melt butter and oil in large frying pan; cook patties, in batches, until browned both sides. Serve with crispy bacon and spinach leaves, if desired.

makes 12
preparation time 25 minutes
cooking time 30 minutes
per patty 9.6g fat; 763kJ (182 cal)

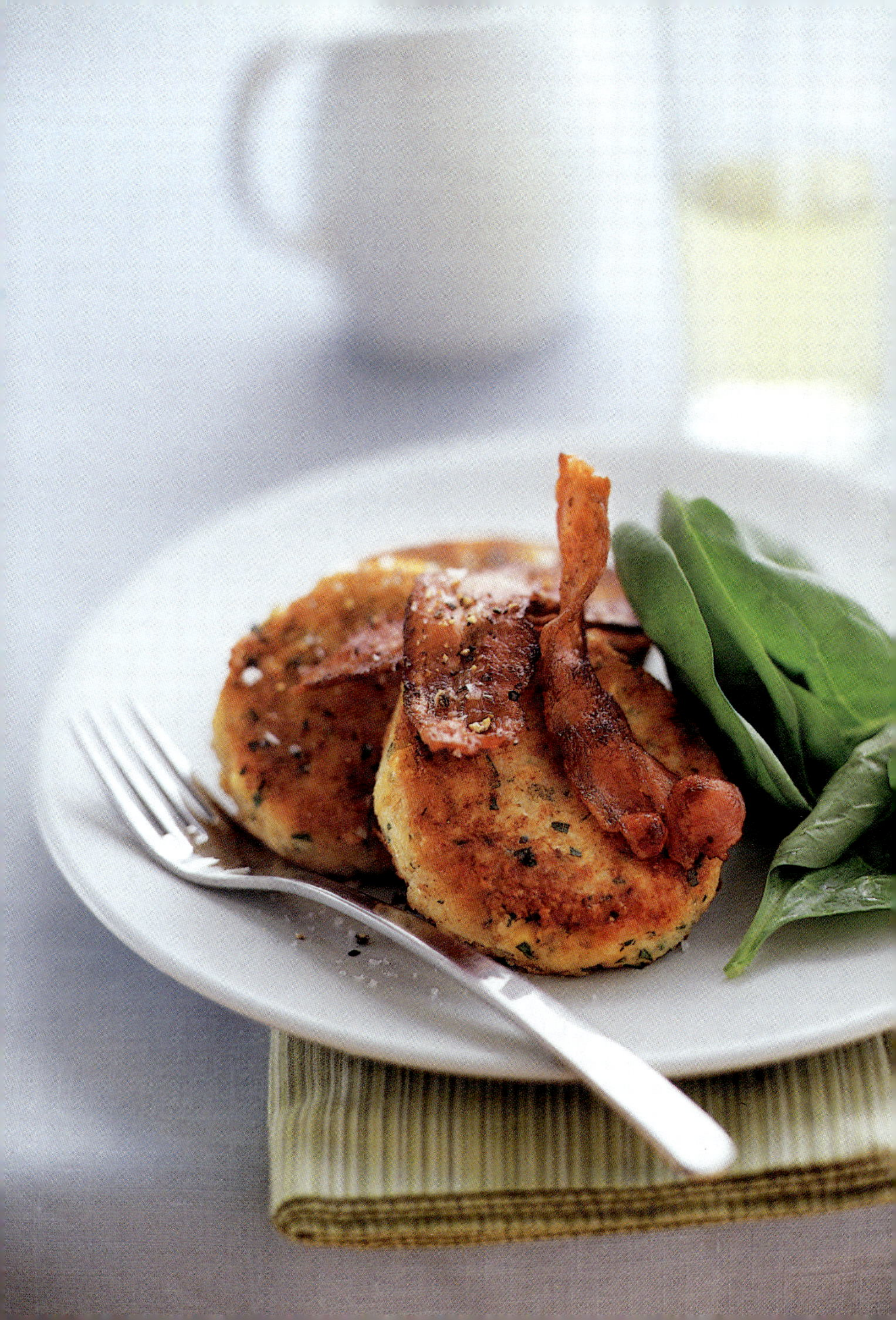

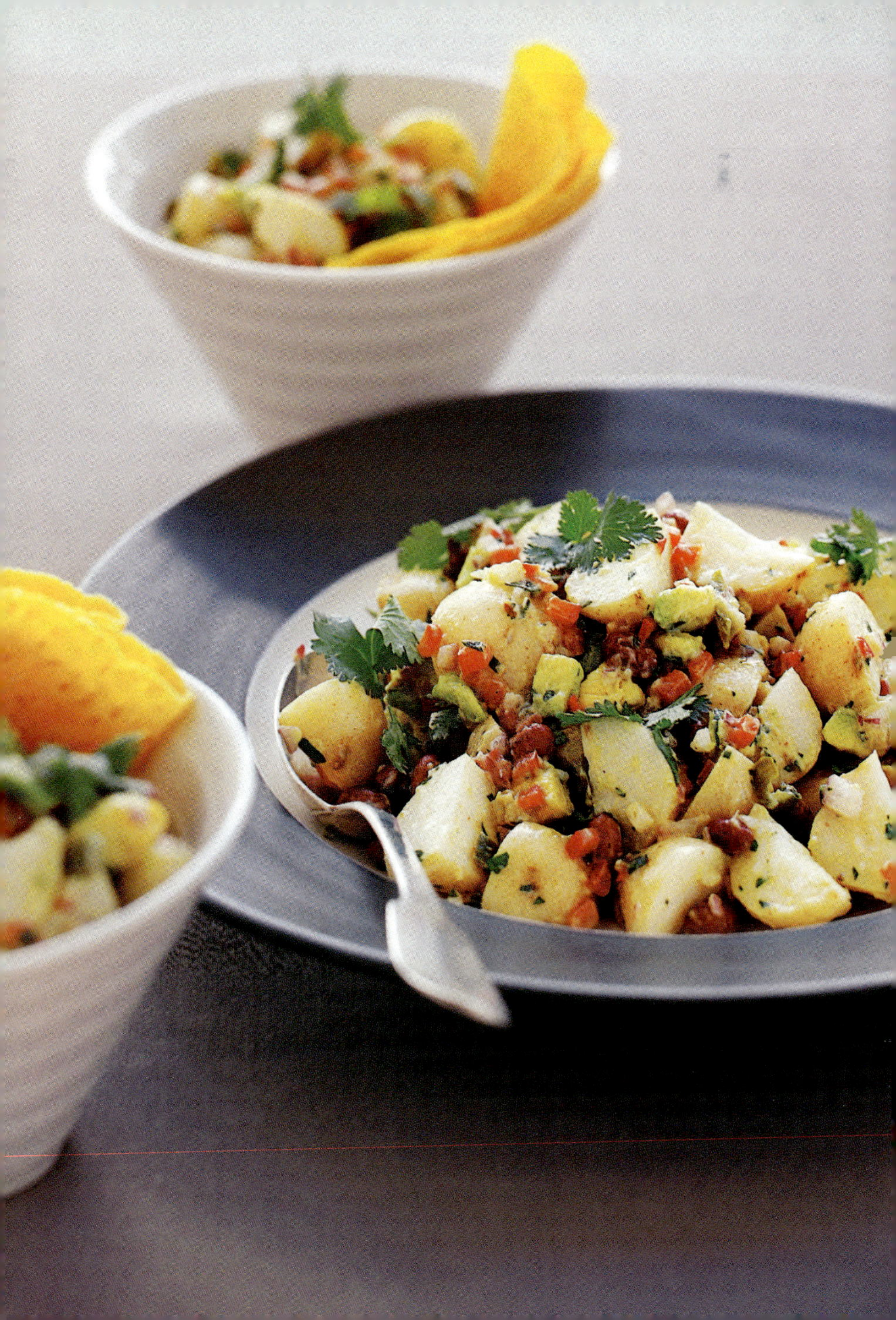

mexican bean potato salad

1kg baby new potatoes, unpeeled, quartered
1 tablespoon lime juice
2 tablespoons vegetable oil
⅓ cup (80g) sour cream
2 cloves garlic, crushed
300g can kidney beans, rinsed, drained
1 small red onion (100g), chopped finely
2 tablespoons finely chopped fresh flat-leaf parsley
2 tablespoons drained bottled sliced jalapeño chillies, chopped coarsely
1 small red capsicum (150g), chopped finely
1 large avocado (320g), chopped finely
1 cup loosely packed fresh coriander leaves
250g package corn tortillas, warmed

1 Boil, steam or microwave potato until just tender; drain. Cover; refrigerate 30 minutes.
2 Meanwhile, combine juice, oil, sour cream and garlic in screw-top jar; shake well.
3 Combine beans, onion, parsley, chilli, capsicum, avocado and coriander in large bowl.
4 Add potato to bean mixture; pour dressing over salad, toss gently to combine. Serve with tortillas.

serves 6
preparation time 20 minutes (plus refrigeration time)
cooking time 15 minutes
per serving 21.4g fat; 1757kJ (420 cal)

ham and black bean soup

Ask your butcher to cut the ham bone in half for you so it fits more easily into the pan.

2½ cups (500g) dried black beans
1kg ham bone
¼ cup (60ml) olive oil
2 medium brown onions (300g), chopped finely
1 medium red capsicum (200g), chopped finely
4 cloves garlic, crushed
1 tablespoon ground cumin
1 teaspoon dried chilli flakes
400g can chopped tomatoes
2.5 litres (10 cups) water
1 tablespoon dried oregano
2 teaspoons ground black pepper
¼ cup (60ml) lime juice
2 medium tomatoes (300g), chopped finely
¼ cup coarsely chopped fresh coriander

1 Place beans in medium bowl, cover with water; stand overnight, drain. Rinse under cold water; drain.
2 Preheat oven to 220°C/200°C fan-forced.
3 Roast ham bone on oven tray, uncovered, 30 minutes.
4 Meanwhile, heat oil in large saucepan; cook onion, capsicum and garlic, stirring, about 5 minutes or until vegetables soften. Add cumin and chilli; cook, stirring, 1 minute. Add beans and ham bone to pan with undrained tomatoes, the water, oregano and pepper; bring to a boil. Reduce heat; simmer, uncovered, 1½ hours.
5 Remove ham bone from soup; shred ham from bone. Discard bone; add ham to soup, stirring until heated through. Stir juice, tomato and coriander into soup just before serving.

serves 8
preparation time 30 minutes (plus standing time)
cooking time 2 hours 15 minutes
per serving 7.3g fat; 650kJ (155 cal)
tip Mash half the beans, then return to the soup, to give it a smoother, almost velvet-like, consistency.

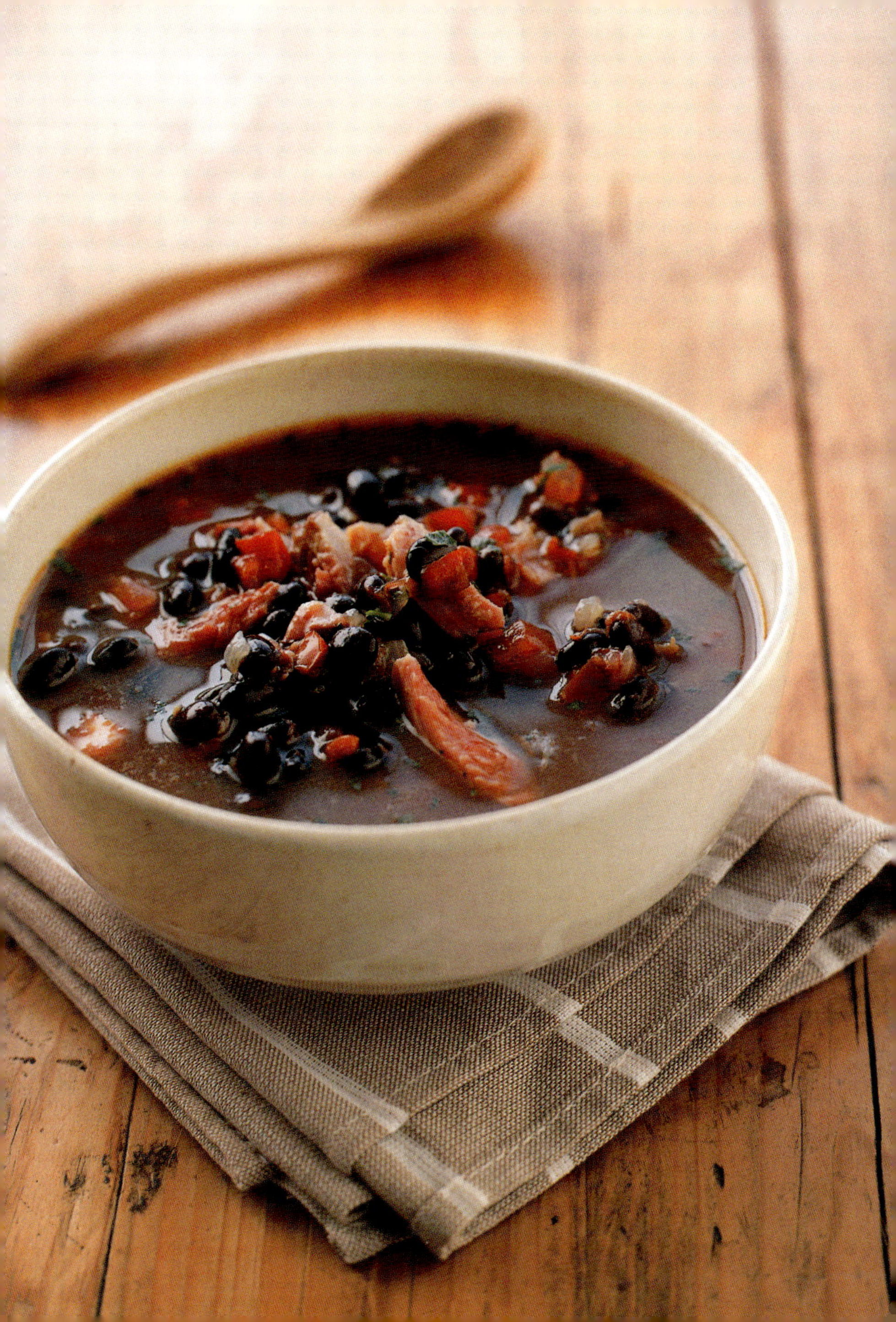

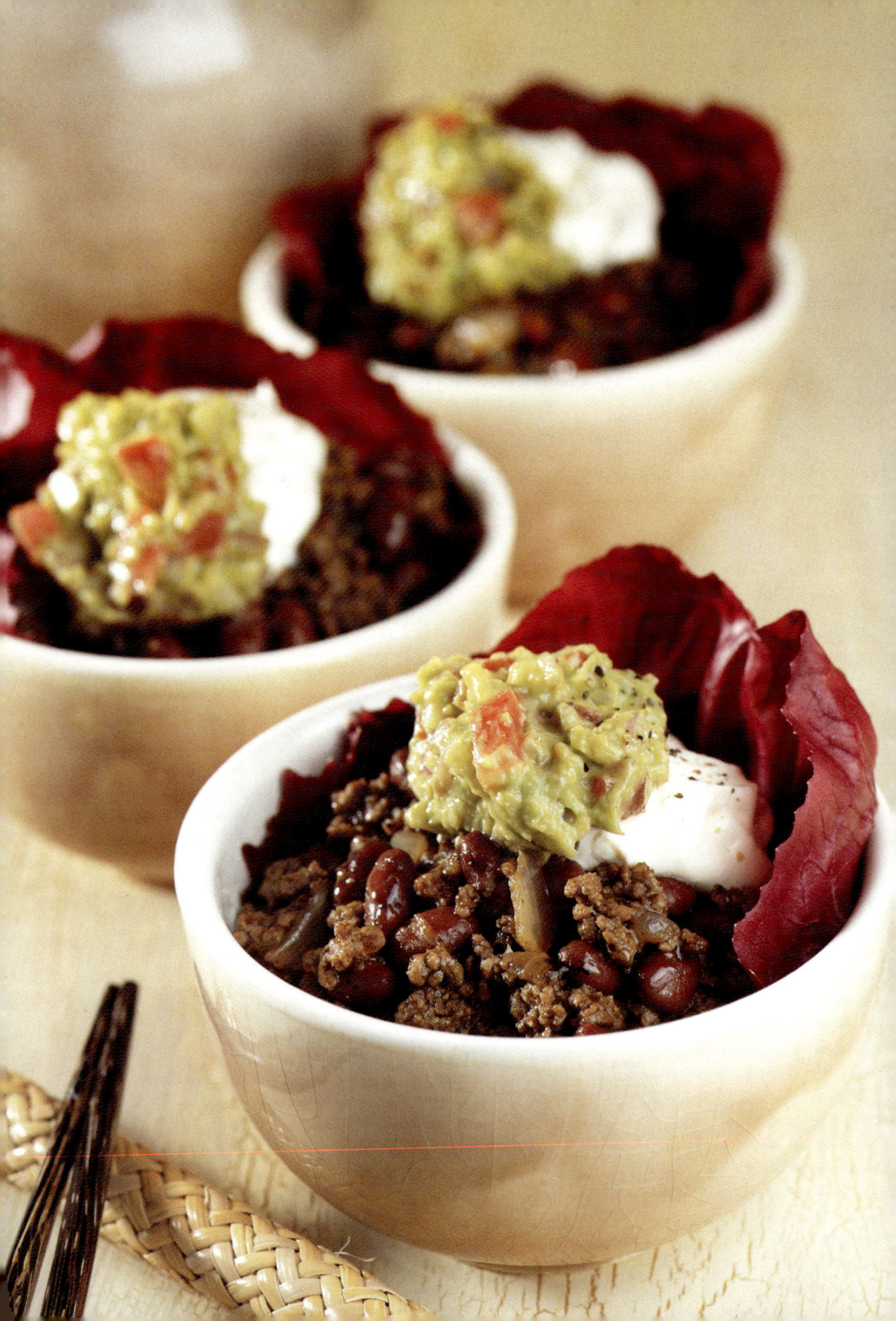

chilli beef 'n' beans **in radicchio cups**

1 medium avocado (250g)
2 tablespoons lime juice
1 small red onion (100g), chopped finely
1 small tomato (130g), seeded, chopped finely
1 tablespoon olive oil
500g minced beef
1 medium brown onion (150g), chopped finely
2 cloves garlic, crushed
2 teaspoons ground coriander
1 fresh small red thai chilli, chopped finely
200g jar taco sauce
290g can kidney beans, rinsed, drained
1 medium radicchio (200g)
½ cup (125ml) sour cream

1 Mash avocado flesh in small bowl until almost smooth; stir in juice, red onion and tomato. Cover avocado mixture; refrigerate.
2 Heat oil in wok; stir-fry beef, brown onion, garlic, coriander and chilli, until beef is browned.
3 Add sauce and beans; stir-fry, stirring until sauce boils.
4 Spoon mixture into radicchio leaves; top with sour cream and avocado mixture.

serves 4
preparation time 15 minutes
cooking time 15 minutes
per serving 38.9g fat; 2353kJ (563 cal)
tip We used a 200g jar of mild taco sauce in this recipe, however, you can use medium or hot versions, if you prefer.

prawns in basil with avocado mash

1kg uncooked tiger prawns
½ cup coarsely chopped fresh basil leaves
2 cloves garlic, crushed
1 tablespoon finely grated lime rind
2 tablespoons peanut oil

avocado mash

2 medium avocados (500g)
2 tablespoons lime juice
2 medium tomatoes (380g), seeded, chopped coarsely
1 small red onion (100g), chopped coarsely
2 teaspoons ground cumin
2 tablespoons coarsely chopped fresh basil
2 fresh small red thai chillies, chopped finely

1 Shell and devein prawns, leaving tails intact. Combine prawns in large bowl with basil, garlic and rind; cover, refrigerate 3 hours or overnight.
2 Heat oil in wok; stir-fry prawns until just changed in colour.
3 Meanwhile, make avocado mash.
4 Serve prawns over avocado mash.
avocado mash Mash flesh of 1 avocado in small bowl until almost smooth. Chop flesh of second avocado roughly; add to bowl of mashed avocado with remaining ingredients, mix well.

serves 4
preparation time 25 minutes (plus refrigeration time)
cooking time 15 minutes
per serving 29.8g fat; 1687kJ (404 cal)

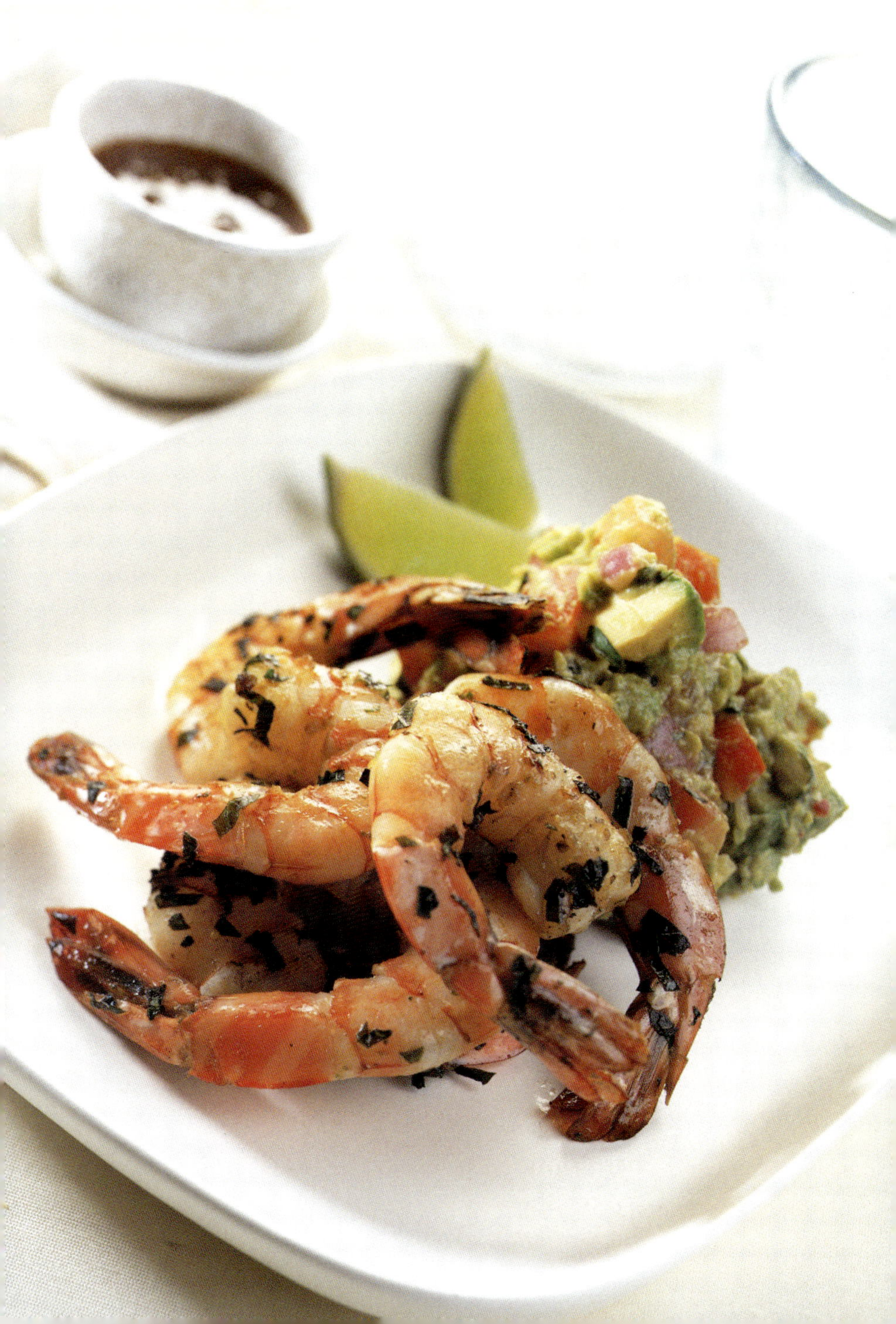

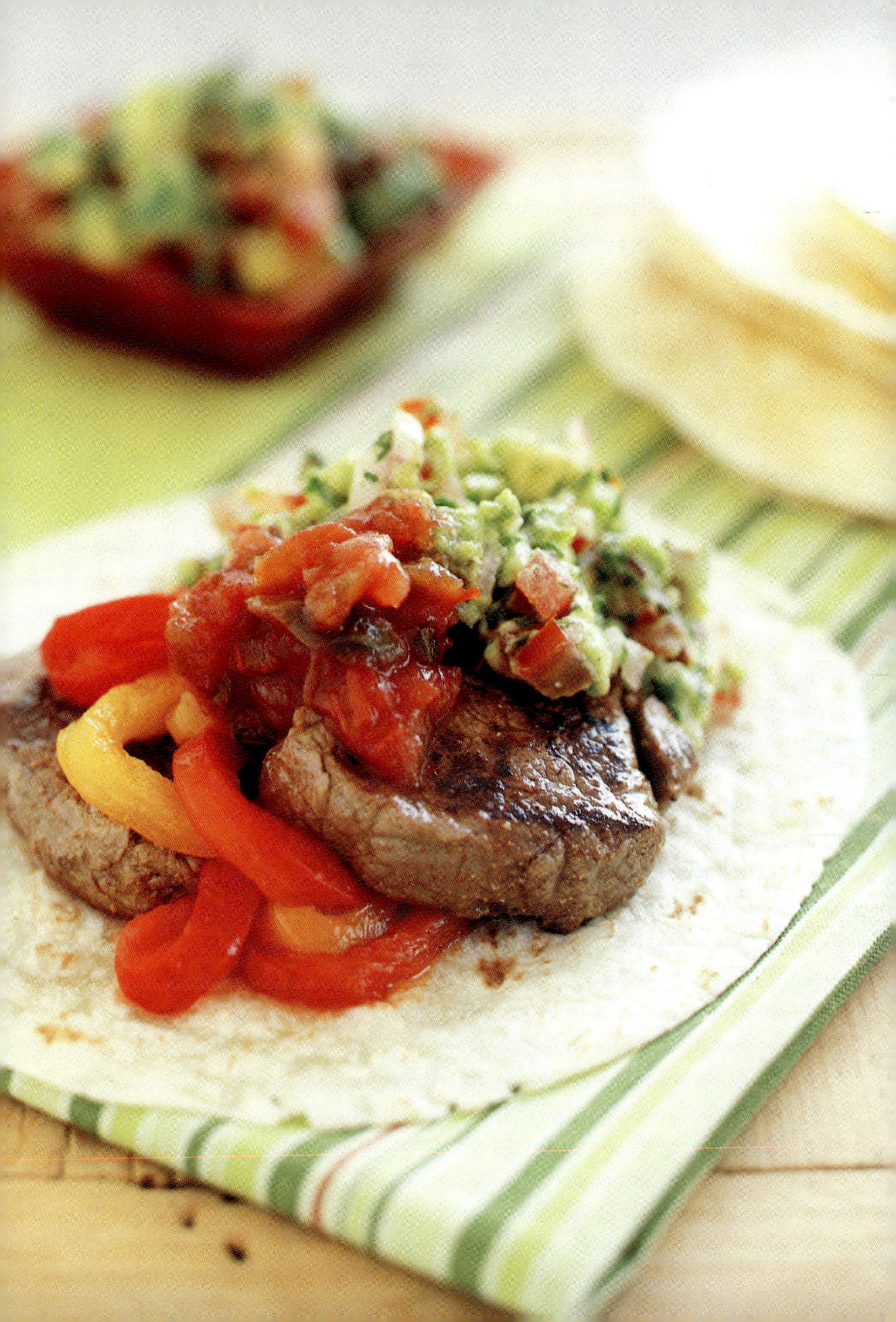

fajitas and guacamole

600g piece scotch fillet
2 cloves garlic, crushed
¼ cup (60ml) lemon juice
1½ teaspoons ground cumin
½ teaspoon cayenne pepper
2 tablespoons olive oil
1 medium yellow capsicum (200g)
1 medium red capsicum (200g)
12 small flour tortillas
375g jar chunky salsa

guacamole
2 medium avocados (500g)
2 medium tomatoes (380g), seeded, chopped finely
1 small red onion (100g), chopped finely
2 tablespoons lime juice
2 tablespoons coarsely chopped fresh coriander

1 Cut beef into thin 2cm-wide slices; place in medium bowl with garlic, juice, spices and oil, toss to coat beef in marinade. Cover; refrigerate 3 hours.
2 Quarter capsicums; remove seeds and membranes. Roast capsicum under grill or in very hot oven, skin-side up, until skin blisters and blackens. Cover with plastic or paper for 5 minutes. Peel away skin; cut capsicums into thin strips.
3 Cook beef, in batches, on heated oiled grill plate (or grill or barbecue) until browned all over and cooked as desired; cover to keep warm.
4 Meanwhile, make guacamole.
5 Reheat capsicum strips on heated grill.
6 Serve tortillas topped with beef, capsicum guacamole and salsa.

guacamole Mash avocados roughly in medium bowl; add remaining ingredients, mix to combine.

serves 4
preparation time 15 minutes (plus refrigeration time)
cooking time 20 minutes
per serving 48.8g fat; 4097kJ (979 cal)
tip Scotch fillet bought in a large piece is also known as rib-eye roast; you can also use rump steak for this recipe.

chilli chicken with corn chips

40g butter
440g chicken thigh fillets, chopped finely
1 cup (250ml) tomato puree
½ cup (125ml) mild chilli sauce
1 tablespoon finely chopped fresh parsley
200g packet cheese-flavoured corn chips
1 cup (125g) coarsely grated tasty cheddar cheese
1 tablespoon finely chopped fresh flat-leaf parsley, extra
4 green onions, chopped finely

1 Heat butter in large saucepan; cook chicken, stirring, until browned all over.
2 Stir in puree, sauce and parsley; simmer about 5 minutes or until sauce is thickened and chicken is cooked through.
3 Preheat grill.
4 Place corn chips in large flameproof dish; top with chicken mixture, sprinkle with cheese. Grill until cheese is melted; serve sprinkled with extra parsley and onion.

serves 4
preparation time 15 minutes
cooking time 20 minutes
per serving 42.2g fat; 2752kJ (657 cal)

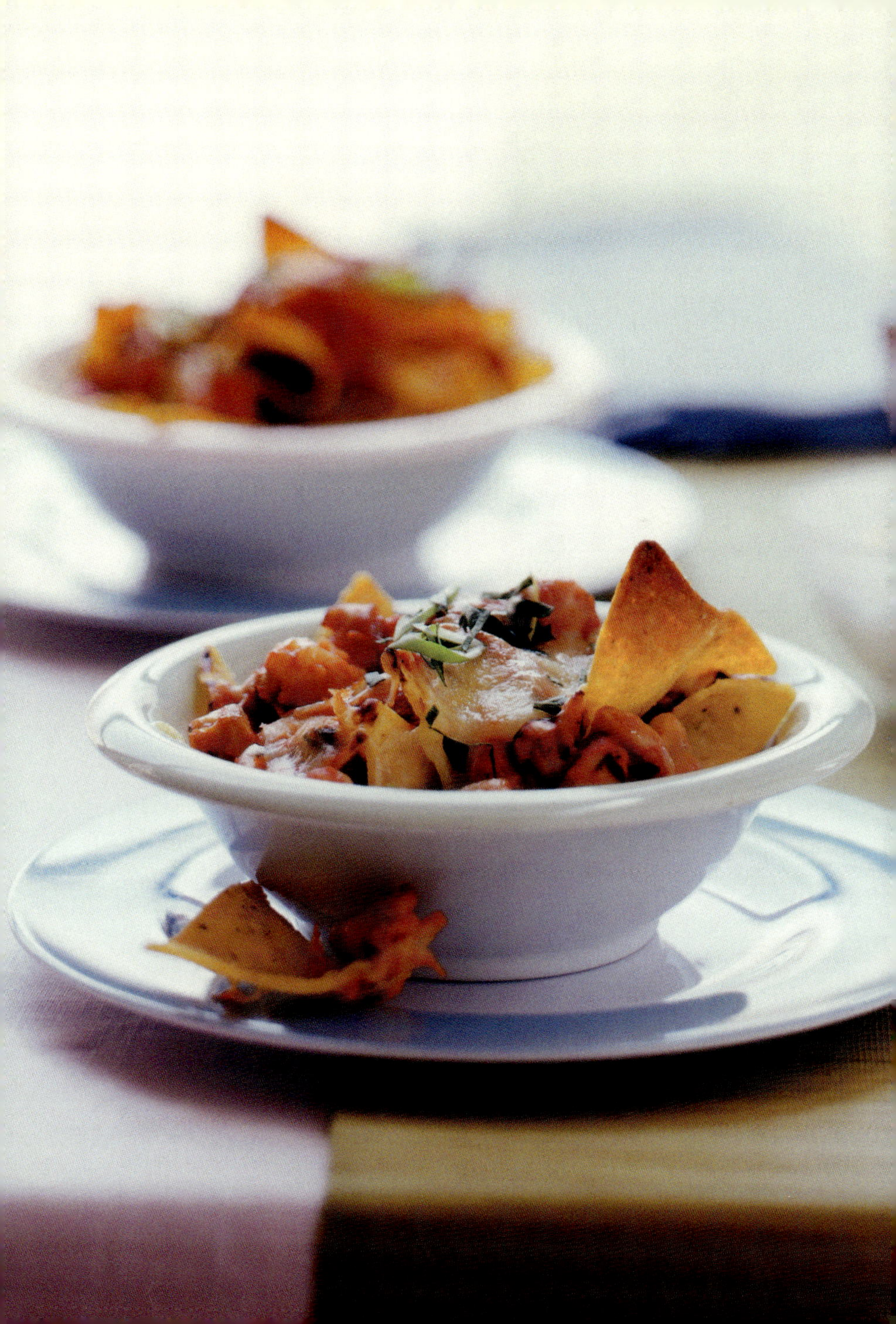

glossary

baking powder a raising agent consisting mainly of two parts cream of tartar to one part bicarbonate of soda (baking soda).

basil an aromatic herb. There are many types; the most commonly used is sweet, or common, basil.

beans
black also known as turtle beans; jet black with a tiny white eye, they are found in most greengrocers and delicatessens. They have a creamy texture and sweet flavour. Not the same as chinese black beans, which are fermented soy beans.
kidney medium-size red bean, slightly floury, sweet flavour; sold dried or canned.

breadcrumbs, fresh bread, usually white, processed into crumbs.

butter use salted or unsalted (sweet) butter; 125g is equal to one stick of butter.

buttermilk sold alongside fresh milk products in supermarkets; originally the liquid left after cream was separated from milk, today, it is commercially made similarly to yogurt.

capsicum also known as bell pepper or, simply, pepper. Native to Central and South America, they can be red, green, yellow, orange or purplish-black. Discard seeds and membranes before use.

cayenne pepper a long, thin-fleshed, extremely hot red chilli usually sold dried and ground.

cheese
cottage fresh, unripened white curd cheese with a grainy consistency.
fontina a smooth firm cheese with a nutty taste and a brown or red rind.
mozzarella a soft, spun-curd cheese. It has a low melting point and a wonderfully elastic texture when heated.

chicken drumettes small, fleshy section of a chicken wing between the shoulder and "elbow"; the meat is scraped down the bone to make a "handle".

chickpeas also called garbanzos, hummus or channa; an irregularly round, sandy-coloured legume.

chilli use rubber gloves when seeding and chopping fresh chillies as they can burn your skin. Removing seeds and membranes lessens the heat level.

chipotle are what fresh jalapeño chillies are called after they've been dried and smoked. Having a deep, intensely smoky flavour rather than a searing heat, chipotles are dark brown, almost black in appearance; they are available from specialty spice stores and gourmet delicatessens.

flakes, dried dehydrated chilli slices and seeds.
guajillo sometimes called travieso ("impish", because its heat can be deceiving) or cascabel ("little bell", because its dried seeds rattle when the chilli is shaken) it is the dried form of the fresh mirasol chilli. So deep-red in colour it is almost black, with a medium-hot heat; must be soaked in boiling water before being used.
jalapeño fairly hot green chilli, available in brine, bottled, or fresh from specialty greengrocers.
thai red also known as "scuds"; tiny, very hot and bright red in colour.

coriander also known as cilantro or chinese parsley; bright-green leafy herb with a pungent flavour. Also sold as seeds, whole or ground.

cumin also known as zeera or comino; has a spicy, nutty flavour. Available as seeds, dried and ground.

five-spice powder a fragrant mix of ground cinnamon, cloves, star anise, sichuan pepper and fennel seeds. Also known as chinese five-spice powder.

flour
plain an all-purpose flour made from wheat.
self-raising plain flour sifted with baking powder in the proportion of 1 cup flour to 2 teaspoons baking powder.

mexican seasoning mix a packaged seasoning meant to duplicate mexican flavours made from oregano, cumin, chillies and other spices.

mexican-style beans are a mildly spiced canned combination of red kidney or pinto beans, capsicum and tomato.

mince meat also known as ground meat, as in beef, veal, pork, lamb and chicken.

oil

olive made from ripened olives. *Extra virgin* and *virgin* are the best, while *extra light* or *light* refers to taste not fat levels.

peanut pressed from ground peanuts; has a high smoke point (capacity to handle high heat without burning).

vegetable any of a number of oils sourced from plants rather than animal fats.

onion

green also known as scallion or, incorrectly, shallot; an immature onion picked before the bulb has formed, having a long, bright-green edible stalk.

spring onions with small white bulbs, long green leaves and narrow green-leafed tops.

red also known as spanish, red spanish or bermuda onion; a sweet-flavoured, large, purple-red onion.

paprika ground dried red capsicum (bell pepper).

parsley, flat-leaf also known as continental or italian parsley.

pearl barley barley that has had its outer husk (bran) removed, and been steamed and polished, much the same as rice.

peppercorns, black is picked when the berry is not quite ripe, then dried until it shrivels and the skin turns dark brown to black. It's the strongest flavoured of all the peppercorn varieties.

polenta a flour-like cereal made of ground corn (maize); similar to cornmeal but finer and lighter in colour; also the name of the dish made from it.

prawns also known as shrimp.

puff pastry, frozen ready-rolled packaged sheets of frozen puff pastry, available from supermarkets.

radicchio a member of the chicory family. Has dark burgundy leaves and a strong bitter flavour.

sausage, chorizo originally from Spain; made of coarsely ground pork and highly seasoned with garlic and chillies.

spinach also known as english spinach and, incorrectly, silver beet.

stock available in cans, bottles or tetra packs. Stock cubes or powder can also be used.

taco seasoning mix see mexican seasoning mix.

tomatoes

cherry also known as tiny tim or tom thumb; small and round.

egg also called plum or roma; smallish and oval-shaped.

pasta sauce, bottled a prepared sauce made of a blend of tomatoes, herbs and spices.

puree canned pureed tomatoes (not tomato paste). Substitute with fresh peeled and pureed tomatoes.

yellow teardrop small yellow pear-shaped tomatoes.

tortilla thin, round unleavened bread originating in Mexico. Two kinds are available, one made from wheat flour and the other from corn.

turmeric a rhizome related to galangal and ginger; must be grated or pounded to release its somewhat acrid aroma and pungent flavour.

vinegar

balsamic originally from Modena, Italy, there are now many balsamic vinegars on the market ranging in quailty and pungency depending on how long they have been aged. Quality can be determined up to a point by price; use the most expensive sparingly.

white wine made from white wine.

zucchini also known as courgette.

conversion chart

MEASURES

One Australian metric measuring cup holds approximately 250ml, one Australian metric tablespoon holds 20ml, one Australian metric teaspoon holds 5ml.

The difference between one country's measuring cups and another's is within a 2- or 3-teaspoon variance, and will not affect your cooking results. North America, New Zealand and the United Kingdom use a 15ml tablespoon. All cup and spoon measurements are level. The most accurate way of measuring dry ingredients is to weigh them. When measuring liquids, use a clear glass or plastic jug with metric markings.

We use large eggs with an average weight of 60g.

DRY MEASURES

METRIC	IMPERIAL
15g	½oz
30g	1oz
60g	2oz
90g	3oz
125g	4oz (¼lb)
155g	5oz
185g	6oz
220g	7oz
250g	8oz (½lb)
280g	9oz
315g	10oz
345g	11oz
375g	12oz (¾lb)
410g	13oz
440g	14oz
470g	15oz
500g	16oz (1lb)
750g	24oz (1½lb)
1kg	32oz (2lb)

LIQUID MEASURES

METRIC	IMPERIAL
30ml	1 fluid oz
60ml	2 fluid oz
100ml	3 fluid oz
125ml	4 fluid oz
150ml	5 fluid oz (¼ pint/1 gill)
190ml	6 fluid oz
250ml	8 fluid oz
300ml	10 fluid oz (½ pint)
500ml	16 fluid oz
600ml	20 fluid oz (1 pint)
1000ml (1 litre)	1¾ pints

LENGTH MEASURES

METRIC	IMPERIAL
3mm	⅛in
6mm	¼in
1cm	½in
2cm	¾in
2.5cm	1in
5cm	2in
6cm	2½in
8cm	3in
10cm	4in
13cm	5in
15cm	6in
18cm	7in
20cm	8in
23cm	9in
25cm	10in
28cm	11in
30cm	12in (1ft)

OVEN TEMPERATURES

These oven temperatures are only a guide for conventional ovens. For fan-forced ovens, check the manufacturer's manual.

	°C (CELSIUS)	°F (FAHRENHEIT)	GAS MARK
Very slow	120	250	½
Slow	150	275 – 300	1 – 2
Moderately slow	160	325	3
Moderate	180	350 – 375	4 – 5
Moderately hot	200	400	6
Hot	220	425 – 450	7 – 8
Very hot	240	475	9

index

A
avocado mash 54

B
bean nachos 13
beef fajitas 26
beef 'n' beans in radicchio cups, chilli 53
beef salad, mexican, with fresh corn salsa 33
beef, mexican 22
beef, stir-fried mexican 41
black bean and lamb soup 45

C
chicken enchiladas with corn salsa 5
chicken, chilli, with corn chips 58
chicken, mexican, with black bean and barley salad 30
chicken, sweet paprika, with tomato and chickpea salsa 37
chickpea corn enchiladas 17
chile con frijoles 18
chilli beef 'n' beans in radicchio cups 53
chilli chicken with corn chips 58
chilli con carne with jalapeño corn muffins 9
chilli con carne, penne with 29
chilli tomato salsa 2
chorizo taquitos with chilli tomato salsa 2
corn and lime salsa 38
corn and zucchini fritters with salsa 14
corn salsa 5
corn salsa, fresh 33
creamed corn and potato patties 46

E
empanadas 10
enchiladas suizas 34
enchiladas, chicken, with corn salsa 5
enchiladas, chickpea corn 17

F
fajitas and guacamole 57
fajitas, beef 26
fresh corn salsa 33
fresh tomato salsa 26, 34
fresh tomato salsa 34
frijoles, chile con 18
fritters, corn and zucchini with salsa 14
fritters, prawn, with avocado salsa 21

G
guacamole 57

H
ham and black bean soup 50

J
jalapeño corn muffins 9

L
lamb and black bean soup 45
lime and corn salsa 38

M
mash, avocado 54
mexican bean potato salad 49
mexican beef 22
mexican beef salad with fresh corn salsa 33
mexican chicken with black bean and barley salad 30
mexican tortilla soup 42
muffins, jalapeño corn 9

N
nachos, bean 13

P
patties, creamed corn and potato 46
penne with chilli con carne 29
prawn fritters with avocado salsa 21

prawn quesadillas with corn and lime salsa 38
prawns in basil with avocado mash 54
prawns, salt and pepper 6

Q
quesadillas, prawn, with corn and lime salsa 38
quesadillas, spinach and cheese 25

S
salad, black bean and barley, mexican chicken with 30
salad, mexican bean potato 49
salad, mexican beef, with fresh corn salsa 33
salsa 14
salsa, avocado, prawn fritters with 21
salsa, chilli tomato 2
salsa, corn 5
salsa, corn and lime 38
salsa, fresh corn 33
salsa, fresh tomato 26, 34
salsa, tomato and chickpea, sweet paprika chicken with 37
salt and pepper prawns 6
soup, black bean and lamb 45
soup, ham and black bean 50
soup, mexican tortilla 42
spinach and cheese quesadillas 25
stir-fried mexican beef 41
sweet paprika chicken with tomato and chickpea salsa 37

T
taquitos, chorizo, with chilli tomato salsa 2
tomato salsa, fresh 26, 34

Z
zucchini and corn fritters with salsa 14

Are you missing some of the world's favourite cookbooks?

The Australian Women's Weekly cookbooks are available from bookshops, cookshops, supermarkets and other stores all over the world. You can also buy direct from the publisher, using the order form below.

MINI SERIES £3.50 190x138MM 64 PAGES

TITLE	QTY	TITLE	QTY	TITLE	QTY
4 Fast Ingredients		Finger Food		Salads	
15-minute Feasts		Gluten-free Cooking		Simple Slices	
50 Fast Chicken Fillets		Healthy Everyday Food 4 Kids		Simply Seafood	
50 Fast Desserts		Ice-creams & Sorbets		Skinny Food	
After-work Stir-fries		Indian Cooking		Spanish Favourites	
Barbecue Chicken		Indonesian Favourites		Stir-fries	
Biscuits, Brownies & Biscotti		Italian Favourites		Summer Salads	
Bites		Jams & Jellies		Tagines & Couscous	
Bowl Food		Japanese Favourites		Tapas, Antipasto & Mezze	
Burgers, Rösti & Fritters		Kids Party Food		Tarts	
Cafe Cakes		Last-minute Meals		Tex-Mex	
Cafe Food		Lebanese Cooking		Thai Favourites	
Casseroles		Low-Fat Delicious		The Fast Egg	
Casseroles & Curries		Low Fat Fast		The Packed Lunch	
Char-grills & Barbecues		Malaysian Favourites		Vegetarian	
Cheesecakes, Pavlova & Trifles		Mince		Vegie Main Meals	
Chinese Favourites		Mince Favourites		Vietnamese Favourites	
Chocolate Cakes		Muffins		Wok	
Christmas Cakes & Puddings		Noodles		Young Chef	
Cocktails		Outdoor Eating			
Crumbles & Bakes		Party Food			
Curries		Pickles and Chutneys			
Dried Fruit & Nuts		Pasta			
Drinks		Potatoes			
Fast Soup		Roast		TOTAL COST	£

Photocopy and complete coupon below

ACP Magazines Ltd Privacy Notice
This book may contain offers, competitions or surveys that require you to provide information about yourself if you choose to enter or take part in any such Reader Offer.
If you provide information about yourself to ACP Magazines Ltd, the company will use this information to provide you with the products or services you have requested, and may supply your information to contractors that help ACP to do this. ACP will also use your information to inform you of other ACP publications, products, services and events. ACP will also give your information to organisations that are providing special prizes or offers, and that are clearly associated with the Reader Offer. Unless you tell us not to, we may give your information to other organisations that use it to inform you about other products, services and events or who may give it to other organisations that may use it for this purpose. If you would like to gain access to the information ACP holds about you, please contact ACP's Privacy Officer at:
ACP Magazines Ltd, 54-58 Park Street, Sydney, NSW 2000, Australia

☐ Privacy Notice: Please do not provide information about me to any organisation not associated with this offer.

Name _____
Address _____
_____ Postcode _____
Country _____ Phone (business hours) _____
Email*(optional) _____
* By including your email address, you consent to receipt of any email regarding this magazine, and other emails which inform you of ACP's other publications, products, services and events, and to promote third party goods and services you may be interested in.

I enclose my cheque/money order for £ _____ or please charge £ _____
to my: ☐ Access ☐ Mastercard ☐ Visa ☐ Diners Club
PLEASE NOTE: WE DO NOT ACCEPT SWITCH OR ELECTRON CARDS

Card number | | | | | | | | | | | | | | | |

3 digit security code *(found on reverse of card)* _____

Cardholder's
signature _____ Expiry date ___ / ___

To order: Mail or fax – photocopy or complete the order form above, and send your credit card details or cheque payable to: Australian Consolidated Press (UK), 10 Scirocco Close, Moulton Park Office Village, Northampton NN3 6AP, phone (+44) (01) 604 642200, fax (+44) (01) 604 642300, e-mail books@acpuk.com or order online at www.acpuk.com
Non-UK residents: We accept the credit cards listed on the coupon, or cheques, drafts or International Money Orders payable in sterling and drawn on a UK bank. Credit card charges are at the exchange rate current at the time of payment.
All pricing current at time of going to press and subject to change/availability.
Postage and packing UK: Add £1.00 per order plus 25p per book.
Postage and packing overseas: Add £2.00 per order plus 50p per book. **Offer ends 31.12.2007**